THE DEPARTMENT OF HOMELAND SECURITY

THE U.S. GOVERNMENT
HOW IT WORKS

★ ★ ★

THE CENTRAL INTELLIGENCE AGENCY
THE DEPARTMENT OF HOMELAND SECURITY
THE FEDERAL BUREAU OF INVESTIGATION
THE HOUSE OF REPRESENTATIVES
THE PRESIDENCY
THE SENATE
THE SUPREME COURT

THE U.S. GOVERNMENT
HOW IT WORKS

THE DEPARTMENT OF HOMELAND SECURITY

RACHEL A. KOESTLER-GRACK

CHELSEA HOUSE
PUBLISHERS
An imprint of Infobase Publishing

The Department of Homeland Security

Copyright ©2007 by Infobase Publishing

Chelsea House
An imprint of Infobase Publishing
132 West 31st Street
New York, NY 10001

ISBN-10: 0-7910-9286-0
ISBN-13: 978-0-7910-9286-6

Library of Congress Cataloging-in-Publication Data

Koestler-Grack, Rachel A., 1973-
  The Department of Homeland Security / Rachel A. Koestler-Grack.
      p. cm. — (The U.S. government: how it works)
  Includes bibliographical references and index.
  ISBN 0-7910-9286-0 (hardcover)
1. United States. Dept. of Homeland Security—Juvenile literature.
2. Terrorism—United States—Prevention—Juvenile literature. 3. National security—United States—Juvenile literature. I. Title. II. Series.

  HV6432.4.K64 2007
  363.325'1560973—dc22

                                    2006028391

Text design by James Scotto-Lavino
Cover design by Ben Peterson

Printed in the United States of America

Bang FOF 10 9 8 7 6 5 4 3 2 1

This book is printed on acid-free paper.

CONTENTS

1

LET'S ROLL

At 7:30 in the morning on September 11, 2001, United Airlines passenger Todd Beamer stood outside the boarding gate of Flight 93. He was engrossed in a conversation with his boss, who was awake early and had called from California. Beamer, who lived in Cranbury, N.J., was headed to California for a business meeting. Usually, he flew Continental, but on this trip, he had chosen United to save his company some money. He pulled the phone away from his ear for a moment. "Is that the final call yet?" he asked the agent at the boarding desk. "No," the agent replied, and he continued his conversation.

It was a picture-perfect morning. Not a single cloud marred the blue September sky that hugged Newark International Airport. The morning ticked along at a comfortable pace, as boarding calls were made and passengers strolled down the jetway onto the plane.

Flight 93's Boeing 757 could carry 182 passengers, but on that morning only 37 people had tickets. Beamer and the other passengers had plenty of room in which to work or to just stretch out and enjoy the flight. As the crew prepared Flight 93 to pull away from the gate, American Airlines Flight 11 departed from Logan International Airport in Boston. Shortly after takeoff, hijackers took over that plane. The pilots of Flight 93, however, were unaware of the trouble onboard Flight 11. Their preflight routine went ahead as normal. Little did

American flags are reflected in a marker inscribed with the words "Let's Roll ..." at a temporary memorial for United Airlines Flight 93 in Shanksville, Pennsylvania. Those words were said by Todd Beamer, a 32-year-old account manager from New Jersey, as the passengers on Flight 93 set off to fight their hijackers.

they or the passengers know that four terrorists armed
with box cutters were seated in first class, praying to
Allah for the mission they were about to undertake.

Soon after Flight 93 took off, the Federal Aviation
Administration (FAA) learned that a second plane,
United Airlines Flight 175, had been hijacked. At once,
United's flight operators began to alert all United flights
of the situation. The message, however, was disturbingly
vague: "Beware cockpit intrusion. Confirm operations
are normal." The captain of Flight 93 confirmed the
transmission, having no idea of the possible danger that
he and his passengers faced.

Minutes later, around 9:30 A.M., the plane reached
35,000 feet. With the course for San Francisco set, the
captain turned on the autopilot. Minutes later, an air-
traffic controller in Cleveland, Ohio, overheard a scuffle
taking place in the Flight 93 cockpit. One pilot screamed,
"Get out of here!" Some more yelling and sounds of a
struggle could be heard. Another angry plea, this time
painfully wounded, called out, "Get out of here!" On the
plane, the terrorists had forced their way into the cockpit,
murdered the pilot and the copilot, and set a course
toward some unknown U.S. landmark.

The air-traffic controller in Cleveland tried to make
contact with the pilot. "United 93, Cleveland," he said.
Raising his voice in concern, he then said, "United 93,
if you hear Cleveland center, [identify yourself] please."
A few moments later, a chilling message came over the
radio. "Ladies and gentlemen here, it's the captain," one

of the hijackers said. "Please sit down. Keep remaining sitting. We have a bomb aboard." The terrorist thought he was speaking to the passengers over the intercom, but he was actually broadcasting over the air-traffic-control frequency.

Meanwhile, in the cabin, some passengers made calls to family members after the hijacking began. Through these calls, they learned about two other hijacked planes that had crashed into the World Trade Center and another that had slammed into the Pentagon. In the past, hijackers had used hostages to get the government to meet their demands. On this day, things were different. This time, the hijackers were using the planes as missiles to take out symbols of American culture and kill thousands of innocent people. Todd Beamer and some of the other passengers decided that their only chance at survival was to fight back.

Knowing that they must act quickly, the passengers devised a plan to overtake their hijackers. Even if they could not save the plane, they would make sure it never hit its intended target. As they prepared to retaliate, Beamer said, "OK. Let's roll."

When the passengers tried to storm the cockpit, the terrorists were taken by surprise. The hijacker piloting the plane rocked the wings back and forth to knock the passengers off their feet. The terrorists soon realized that they would not make it to their destination. "Should we finish it off?" one hijacker asked in Arabic. The pilot flipped the plane upside down and tipped the nose

An FBI aerial photograph, taken on September 12, 2001, shows the crash site of Flight 93 in Pennsylvania. The hijackers steered the plane into the ground once the passengers stormed the cockpit.

toward the ground. As the jet plunged from the sky, the terrorists screamed in Arabic, "Allah is the greatest! Allah is the greatest!" Shortly after 10:00 A.M., Flight 93 crashed into a field in Somerset County, Pennsylvania, southeast of Pittsburgh. All 44 people aboard died in the crash, including the two pilots, five flight attendants, 33 passengers, and four hijackers.

TIME FOR CHANGE

Nearly 3,000 people died in the terrorist attacks of September 11. The events of that day left Americans and people around the world horrified. For many, the shock quickly turned to anger. Who let these terrorists get onboard? Could the attacks have been prevented?

At the time, hijacking a plane was relatively easy. Airport screeners often were barely trained and poorly paid. Even if the screeners had been more alert, though, knives under four inches long and box cutters, which were reportedly used by the terrorists, were legal to carry on a plane. Cockpit doors were not secured. Undoubtedly, it was time for change.

The U.S. government was faced with the daunting task of fixing the national security system. President George W. Bush and his administration set out to punish the terrorist group responsible for these acts and to find better ways to keep the United States safe. Among the actions was the federal restructuring of the national security system. This move resulted in a whole new government department charged with protecting the nation—the Department of Homeland Security.

2

THE BEGINNINGS OF NATIONAL SECURITY

The federal government defines homeland security as a united, national effort to protect the United States from terrorists. After the attacks of September 11, the government decided that there should be a special department to handle national safety and established the Department of Homeland Security. The concept of national security is not new, and terrorism is certainly not a new phenomenon. The Department of Homeland Security is simply a new name for an old mission.

Many Americans think that the 9/11 attacks ushered in a whole new danger to the country. In truth, Americans of every generation have experienced some worry that they might be attacked in their homes. Even the first colonists feared for their safety. In those days, protecting the homeland mainly meant defending towns and borders from Native Americans. Today, modern technology allows terrorists to wreak havoc on a much wider scale, but the country's early experiences were the first indications of a need for national security.

Throughout history, America has experienced many terrorist threats, at home and abroad. In the early years, the United States had to protect itself from land-hungry countries that wanted a piece of North America for themselves. Eventually, these threats against the coastline and borders diminished, but a new type of danger replaced them—domestic terrorism.

HOMEGROWN TERROR

Over the years, there have been many domestic threats, or threats within the United States. By definition, domestic terrorism is an act of violence committed by a group without foreign influence or support against the criminal laws of the United States, intended to intimidate the public or influence government policies. Throughout U.S. history, domestic terrorism has been the most common form of terrorism in the country and until September 11, 2001, the most deadly. From 1980 to 2001, the Federal Bureau of Investigation (FBI) recorded 264 cases of domestic terrorism in the United States. During the same period, the FBI recorded just 89 cases of international terrorism in the country.

These types of attacks first surfaced before, during, and after the Civil War (1861–1865). In the mid-1800s, tensions mounted between people in the Northern and Southern regions of the United States. People in each of these areas had quite different lifestyles. In the North, the economy was based on industry and growing food crops to be sold in the United States. Southerners depended solely on agriculture and crops sold mainly for export, like cotton and tobacco. Southern plantation owners used African-American slaves to work in their large fields. Many northerners, though, opposed slavery. In fact, slavery was illegal in many Northern states.

At the time, the United States was also deciding what to do about the issue of slavery in the new Western territories. These territories had not yet been divided into states, and the government had to determine if slavery would be legal or illegal in these areas. During the presidential election of 1860, Abraham Lincoln promised that, if he were elected, he would not expand slavery into the new territories. Naturally, Lincoln's position enraged Southern politicians and plantation owners, who felt as if their economy and way of life were being threatened. When Lincoln won the election, people from South Carolina decided that they no longer wanted to be governed by U.S. laws and seceded from the Union. By February 1861, six more states joined South Carolina—Mississippi, Alabama, Georgia, Florida, Louisiana, and Texas. They decided to form a new nation called the Confederate States of America. President Lincoln refused to acknowledge the Confederate government and insisted that the states still belonged to the Union. The Confederate states, however, were determined to rule themselves, and on April 12, Confederate soldiers took control of Fort Sumter in South Carolina. Suddenly, the new Confederacy was a looming threat to the safety of the United States.

The battle at Fort Sumter marked the beginning of the Civil War. After that battle, Virginia, North Carolina, Tennessee, and Arkansas also joined the Confederacy. The Union was forced to fight against other Americans. Besides major military attacks, the Union home front also faced raids, draft riots, espionage, and sabotage. On one occasion, Confederate spies tried to burn down New York City. In the North, a shrill cry for national security rang out. In response, Congress suspended the right of habeas corpus, which requires police officers to provide solid proof against a suspect before a judge will hold him prisoner. The government also prosecuted U.S. civilians in military tribunals, a kind of military court designed to try members of enemy forces during wartime. These courts are judged by military officers, who also serve as the jurors. By taking these measures, the Union hoped to catch and punish rebels before they could do harm to U.S. citizens. It was the first time in history that the United States was forced to take such drastic measures to help keep the country safe.

After the Civil War and into the early 1900s, the United States witnessed dramatic episodes of terrorism at home. In the South and other places in the country,

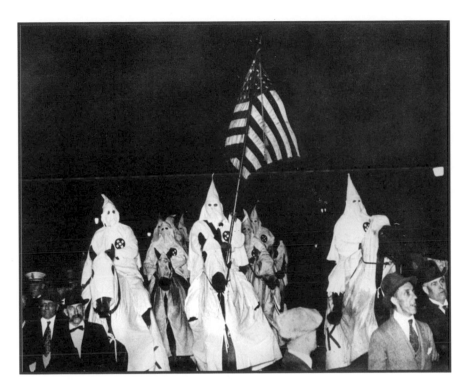

After the Civil War and throughout much of the twentieth century, the Ku Klux Klan terrorized African Americans. Here, the Klan parades through the streets of Tulsa, Oklahoma, in September 1923.

the Ku Klux Klan terrorized African Americans. This hate group set fire to houses, bombed churches, and senselessly murdered hundreds of African-American men, women, and children. At first, these attacks were treated more as criminal acts than as national threats, but racism could be found all around, and many Americans constantly worried about their safety. Later, during the civil rights movement of the 1960s, racist acts finally became a top national-security priority. State and federal troops stepped in to quiet riots and prevent unlawful and cruel treatment of African Americans.

THE RED SCARE

In the early 1900s, socialists and communists in the United States formed organizations. These groups strongly opposed the U.S. democratic form of government, and loyal citizens considered them anti-American. During World War I (1914–1918), the Socialist Party of America openly opposed the war, and members gave speeches to urge the public to resist the draft. Some socialist leaders also formed labor unions, like the Industrial Workers of the World (IWW). They encouraged miners and railroad workers to go on strike. Some of these strikes erupted into riots. The rising power and influence of communist and socialist leaders ignited a burning anxiety in many Americans. Overseas, communist Russia was ablaze with revolution, and many Americans feared that a similar revolt might take place in the United States. This period of communist threat became known as the Red Scare. Congress quickly passed the Espionage Act of 1917, which made it a crime to convey information that aimed to interfere with the operation or success of the U.S. armed forces. Next, Congress passed the Sedition Act of 1918. This law banned the use of "disloyal, profane, scurrilous, or abusive language" against the government during wartime. It also gave the postmaster general the power to slow or confiscate all mail by government dissenters during wartime.

Some mail slipped through the cracks, however. In April 1919, the mayor of Seattle received a homemade bomb in the mail. The next day, a package addressed to a U.S. senator blew off the hands of the servant who found it. The following morning, a New York City postal worker discovered 16 bomb packages—each containing enough nitroglycerin to kill a person—addressed

People milled about in front of the home of U.S. Attorney General Alexander M. Palmer in Washington, D.C., after an explosion there in 1919. After the bombing, federal authorities started an aggressive pursuit of anarchist, socialist, and communist groups in the country.

to well-known people, including oil tycoon John D. Rockefeller. More than likely, the Sedition Act helped intercept these bombs.

After a bomb exploded at the house of U.S. Attorney General Alexander M. Palmer in June 1919, federal authorities started aggressive investigations of radical political groups. The Red Scare quickly escalated into a crazy paranoia. Federal agents conducted raids in cities across the nation, arresting thousands of suspected radicals, many of them immigrants, many of them innocent.

The violence peaked on September 16, 1920, in New York City. A horse-drawn cart carrying a bomb with 100 pounds (45 kilograms) of dynamite embedded with 500 pounds (227 kilograms) of fragmented steel stopped in front of the offices of the J.P. Morgan Company on Wall Street in Lower Manhattan. The explosion killed 38 people and injured 300 others. Although anarchists were blamed for the attack, the identity of the bombers was never discovered.

Besides passing legislation like the Espionage Act, federal authorities created a security system that included Army and Navy intelligence and the Department of Justice, as well as semi-private volunteer groups like the Minnesota Commission for Public Safety. (This commission, which existed from 1917 to 1919, had broad powers to protect people and property in the state.) This system, although sometimes prone to lash out with vigilante justice, helped to crack down on radical socialists during the Red Scare. Several years after World War I, when the threat of communism diminished, the system and most of the volunteer organizations quickly disbanded. A second Red Scare, however, would rise up only a few decades later.

WORLD WAR II TERROR

Many people compare the 9/11 attacks to the Japanese bombing of Pearl Harbor in 1941. On the morning of December 7, the Imperial Japanese Navy made a surprise attack on Pearl Harbor in Oahu, Hawaii—a U.S. Navy base and headquarters of the U.S. Pacific Fleet. By the end of the battle, 12 American warships were severely damaged or destroyed and 2,335 American servicemen and 68 civilians were killed. The attack immediately pulled the United States into World War II.

Just like on September 11, U.S. citizens were shocked that such a devastating attack went undetected. The federal government jumped to protect America's home front. Congress made wartime efforts to protect ports and other key facilities, including the deployment of 200,000 military police officers to guard more than 16,000 sites and buildings. Millions of citizens signed up for civilian defense organizations that provided surveillance and emergency response units that were even trained for a Nazi chemical attack.

During World War II, however, only a few incursions on American soil took place. In June 1942, German submarines landed eight trained saboteurs on Long Island, New York, and near Jacksonville, Florida. These German agents specialized in sabotage—or destroying enemy buildings, railroads, ships, bridges, and other important structures. They had spent years in the United States—at least two had citizenship—and they carried enough cash and explosives to destroy a number of key facilities across the country. Soon after the saboteurs landed, however, one of them confessed and exposed the others, who were quickly captured. All eight saboteurs were convicted, and six were put to death.

On the West Coast, a seaplane launched from a Japanese submarine dropped a bomb near Brookings, Oregon, in September 1942. After hearing news about the German saboteurs, some Americans began to worry that Japanese spies and saboteurs were also in the United States. A government agency called the War Relocation Authority forcibly moved almost 120,000 Japanese and Japanese Americans on the West Coast to internment camps, or isolated housing camps. Many of these Japanese Americans lost all their belongings and property while they were away, and no one returned their possessions after the war. Years later, the poor treatment of Japanese Americans sparked controversy and debate. Finally, in 1988, President Ronald Reagan made a formal apology to the people held in the internment camps and offered payment to surviving internees. The reparations, though, were not enough to fully cover their losses.

For a few years after World War II, Americans once again relaxed and worried little about threats from overseas. Then, in 1949, the Soviet Union tested its first nuclear weapon. Less than a year later, the Korean War broke out. The conflict began as a civil war between communist North Korea and Western-backed South Korea but escalated into a multinational war. These events lit the fuse of a second Red Scare, more commonly called the Cold War.

The Cold War was not a war fought on battlefields with guns and grenades. It was a phantom-like war over differences in politics, economics, and ideologies between the two post-World War II superpowers—the Soviet Union and the United States—and their allies. Lasting until 1991, the Cold War was a race to be the best and most powerful nation in the world. In one arena, the United States and the Soviet Union competed in a "space race" to be the first country to send a man into outer space and eventually to the moon. The greatest threat of this era grew out of the arms race—a competition to have the most nuclear bombs and traditional weapons, as well as strong military alliances. The ultimate fear of most Americans was that the Cold War would escalate into an all-out nuclear war in which hundreds of millions of people would be killed.

In the name of national security, the U.S. government threw its attention toward the development of the best defense system. In the 1980s, the Department of Defense even started to develop the Strategic Defense Initiative (SDI), which was more commonly called Star Wars after the popular science-fiction movies. The planned SDI system would protect Americans from a nuclear missile that had already been fired by destroying it in space.

During the early years of the Cold War, more concrete defense programs sprang up across the country. Federal, state, and local governments encouraged individuals and communities to build bomb shelters to protect themselves from a Soviet nuclear attack. Congress created the Federal Civil Defense Administration to provide technical assistance to local and state civil defense leaders.

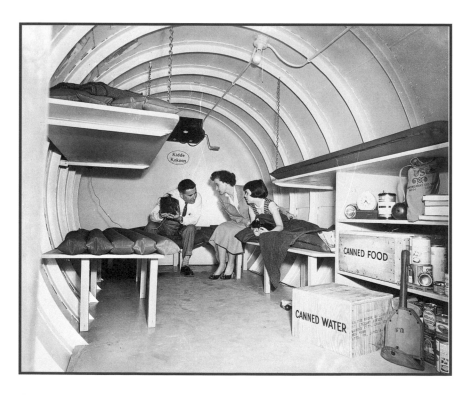

This steel bomb shelter, in a photograph from 1955, had five bunk beds, lanterns, canned food, water, and a radiation detector. During the 1950s, the U.S. government encouraged citizens to build bomb shelters to protect themselves against a feared nuclear attack from the Soviet Union.

The government also established the Office of Defense Mobilization in the Department of Defense. This agency was responsible for stockpiling critical supplies and organizing a plan for quick delivery of these items in the event of a war.

MANY FACES OF TERRORISM

Threats on American soil did not just come from the communists, however. Throughout the 1900s, a range of terrorist groups carried out attacks against the United States. Puerto Rican nationalists, seeking independence from the United States, tried to kill President Harry Truman in 1950, opened fire in the U.S. Capitol in 1954, and launched more attacks in the following decades. In 1963, radical Ku Klux Klan members bombed a church in Birmingham, Alabama, killing four African-American teenagers. Klan beatings and murders continued throughout much of the 1960s. Around this time, domestic terrorism began to take root with groups of protesters who were against the Vietnam War. One of these left-wing terrorist groups, the Weather Underground, bombed the U.S. Capitol in 1971; no one was injured.

By 1975, the number of terrorist groups at work in the United States was overwhelming. When a bomb exploded at LaGuardia Airport in New York City, killing 11 people, the police faced a baffling lineup of suspects. Among those investigated were Puerto Rican nationalists, the Jewish Defense League, the Palestine Liberation Organization (PLO), and Croatian nationalists. The case

THE EXTREMES OF PROTEST

★ ★ ★ ★ ★

Sometimes, terrorist groups can develop from legitimate causes like the environment, animal rights, or the anti-abortion movement. Radicals involved in these issues have been known to resort to domestic terrorism—bombing buildings and threatening the lives of other Americans.

With an intense desire to stop abortion, some extremists have moved beyond peaceful protest. A number of pro-life radicals belong to the Army of God—a group of Christian militants. Across the country, Army of God members have attacked abortion doctors and bombed abortion clinics. In response, the Freedom of Access to Clinic Entrances Act was passed in 1994. It prohibits the use of intimidation or physical force to prevent or discourage people from entering a reproductive-health facility.

Most Americans support protection of the environment and oppose cruelty to animals. Some extremists, though, believe that society does not go far enough. Since 1976, these radicals have committed more than 1,100 criminal acts in the United States, causing at least $110 million in

has never been solved. The FBI, the CIA, and other government agencies ran into a "bureaucratic wall" during their investigation. In the 1970s, the American people discovered that these agencies had used covert tactics and aggressive intelligence against civil rights groups and lawful protesters. These abuses led Congress to place dramatic restrictions on domestic intelligence operations. Decades later, this same wall would hamper investigations of al Qaeda terrorists who were preparing to attack

damages. The Earth Liberation Front demands an end to destruction of the environment. Members started with tree spiking, which involves hammering a metal rod into a tree trunk to discourage logging. They have also destroyed logging equipment, and more recently, they have resorted to arson. Other targets of the Earth Liberation Front include dealerships that sell sport-utility vehicles, construction sites, and even fast-food restaurants.

Founded in Great Britain, the Animal Liberation Front aims to stop what it feels is the exploitation of animals, including the sale of fur items and medical testing on animals. Even though the front claims to abhor acts that could harm any animal—human or nonhuman—it encourages its members to attack targets like fur companies, mink farms, restaurants, and animal research laboratories. Some groups linked to the Animal Liberation Front have committed vandalism, made harassing phone calls and threats, and broken into research labs and set animals free. Some of these disruptions have set back scientists working to find cures for diseases.

the United States. By the 1980s, however, the types of attacks seen in the previous few decades had started to decrease as most of the nationalist and left-wing terrorist groups in the United States fizzled out. Terrorism around the world, though, showed no signs of waning.

3

THE RISE OF MODERN TERRORISM

During the Cold War, modern terrorism was taking root. Although terrorism had been a form of warfare for centuries, the world was introduced to a different type of terrorism after World War II. A distinctive kind of warfare exploded in bursts around the globe. It was called *guerrilla*, after the Spanish word for "little war." Small rebel—or insurgent—units rose up to challenge their country's rulers, often larger colonial governments. These insurgents objected to powerful governments that ruled and exploited smaller countries. Guerrilla fighters saw themselves as legitimate military units, vigilantes for justice who were fighting to muscle foreign powers out of their country.

In the beginning, guerrilla units may have qualified as legitimate armies. They wore uniforms, openly carried their weapons, had a clear command structure, and followed the laws of war. Gradually, however, their methods changed. They began to look for enemy weaknesses to exploit. They would ambush their targets and then escape into the mountains or jungles. They attacked civilians and murdered sympathizers. Inspired by these anti-colonial "freedom fighters," a variety of nationalist and ideological groups picked up arms, and started their own little wars. They turned to hijackings, bombings, and political coups to force their cause. To gain supporters, they used the global media network to spread information against colonial governments.

In the late 1960s, Palestinian groups—outraged by an increasingly dominant Israel—tested the effectiveness of modern terrorism. In June 1967, Israel inflicted a humiliating defeat on its Arab neighbors during the Six-Day War. This defeat set the stage for an era of modern international terrorism. Palestinian guerrillas quickly lost hope that their Arab allies could oust the Israelis, yet they were reluctant to take on the powerful Israeli military directly. Instead, they turned to terrorism. One of the first modern terrorist acts took place on July 22, 1968, when gunmen from the Popular Front for the Liberation of Palestine (PFLP) hijacked an Israeli passenger flight. Thirty-two passengers were held hostage for five weeks. The objectives of the hijackers were to win the release of Palestinian prisoners and to gain worldwide attention. They achieved both.

During the following years, terrorist strikes in Europe rose spectacularly. The most notable attack took place at the 1972 Summer Olympics in Munich, Germany. On September 5, Palestinian terrorists of the "Black September" group, dressed in ski masks, seized 11 Israeli athletes and held them hostage for almost 18 hours in their

At the 1972 Olympics in Munich, Germany, Palestinian terrorists seized 11 members of the Israeli Olympic team, held them hostage, and murdered them during a failed rescue attempt. Here, Andrea Spitzer, the widow of the Israeli Olympic fencing coach, surveys the disorder in the Olympic Village room where the hostages were held. Bullet holes on the wall were outlined in chalk.

apartment in the Olympic Village. During a failed rescue attempt, the captors murdered all the Israeli hostages, and all but three of the terrorists were killed. The event became known as the "Munich massacre."

Yasir Arafat, the leader of the Palestine Liberation Organization (PLO), won a series of diplomatic victories because of the notoriety of the Olympic attack and other terrorist acts. Ultimately, Arafat became an international figure, and Palestinian issues earned a top spot on the world's diplomatic agenda. This prominence might never have happened if Palestinians had used traditional attacks against Israel instead of spectacular terrorist strikes. On the other hand, the PLO failed to achieve two of its major goals—the destruction of Israel and the creation of an independent Palestinian state.

Other areas in the Middle East were not immune to turmoil, and the United States became caught up in the strife. In 1979, Ayatollah Khomeini, an exiled Shiite leader, managed to topple the U.S.-installed Shah of Iran. He heralded America as the "great Satan" and allowed his followers to seize the U.S. Embassy in Tehran and hold 52 hostages for more than a year. Many people liked the charismatic leader and rallied around him, forming a dislike for the United States. His triumph in taking control of the U.S.-created government inspired religious radicals throughout the Middle East. Days after the embassy crisis began, Islamic extremists in Mecca, Saudi Arabia, stormed the Grand Mosque and took hundreds of hostages. And in Libya and Pakistan, mobs burned the U.S. embassies.

A banner depicting President Jimmy Carter as a devil was carried during an anti-American march in November 1979 in Tehran, Iran. Followers of Ayatollah Khomeini seized the U.S. Embassy in Tehran that month and held 52 hostages for more than a year.

The Lebanese group Hizbollah, and its supporters in the Iranian and Syrian governments, found terrorism to be effective during the 1980s. The members of Hizbollah sought to make Lebanon a Shiite state. In 1983, U.S. forces were trying to stabilize Lebanon, and Hizbollah wanted the Americans out of the country. In April, a suicide bomber blew up the U.S. Embassy in Beirut, killing 63 people. The blast was credited to Islamic Jihad, another name for Hizbollah and other Iran-supported terrorist groups. Then, in the early morning of October 23, a yellow Mercedes truck plowed over the concertina-wire barriers at the U.S. Marine barracks near the Beirut airport. The truck roared past two guard posts before soldiers could even get a shot off. When the truck reached the barracks entrance, it crashed through a sandbag barricade and slammed into the building, exploding with the force of 12,000 pounds (5,443 kilograms) of dynamite. The massive blast pulled the building off its foundation, and the walls collapsed inward. Almost simultaneously, another suicide bomber attacked the barracks of French paratroopers. Nearly 300 American and French troops were crushed inside the two barracks under tons of concrete and jagged steel. After a brief military strike-back, the United States pulled its troops out of Lebanon, in an apparent victory for the terrorists.

Next, Hizbollah used hostage tactics. Terrorists seized and sometimes killed U.S. and other Western hostages. As the crisis grew more intense, President Ronald Reagan was forced to break U.S. policies and make a deal with

Iran, the group's primary supporter. He traded weapons for hostages. The U.S. government made pledges to bring Hizbollah to justice for these and other terrorist attacks. Hizbollah, however, continued to be a major player in the region's affairs. Much like the PLO, though, Hizbollah may have achieved short-term victories—like forcing U.S. troops out of Lebanon. Long-term goals, like gaining total political and military control over Lebanon, remain unmet.

The United States denounced state-sponsored terrorist groups backed by nations like Iran, Libya, and Syria. By 1986, the United States had placed economic sanctions on those three countries and had launched military strikes against Libya. Unfortunately, these responses did not stop state-sponsored terrorists. In 1988, the police arrested a Japanese citizen at a New Jersey rest stop after they found three bombs in his car. It was later revealed that the man was working for Libyan terrorists and planned to strike New York City. Later that year, in an attack linked to Libya, Pan Am Flight 103 exploded over Lockerbie, Scotland, killing 270 people. Still, the United States asserted that the main terrorist threat was to Americans abroad, not at home. Also, the U.S. government was more interested in the breakup of the Soviet Union. Officials believed that the collapse of the Soviet Union would weaken state-sponsored terrorists. The decline of state-sponsored terrorism, however, was what ultimately gave rise to Osama bin Laden and helped pave the road to the September 11 attacks.

Beginning in 1979, the Soviet Union became embroiled in a war in Afghanistan. Soviet forces were fighting anti-government insurgents who opposed the Soviet-backed Afghan government. The war dragged on for nine years, a fight that the Soviet government could not afford. In 1988, the Soviets began to withdraw from Afghanistan, leaving behind thousands of foreign holy warriors who had traveled from all over the world to fight communism in support of radical Islam. They were hungry to continue their battle. Around this time, a 6-foot, 6-inch militant Islamist stepped in to guide these Arabs toward their next fight. This Saudi multimillionaire, Osama bin Laden,

Anti-Soviet Afghan resistance fighters are seen with their primitive weapons in the eastern part of Afghanistan. After the Soviets withdrew from Afghanistan in the late 1980s, thousands of foreign holy warriors who fought the communists were left behind. Many of these men, who supported radical Islam, fell under the sway of Osama bin Laden.

began to form an organization of militants, which he called al Qaeda, or "the base," after a training camp in Afghanistan. He went on to mold the group into an extensive Islamic terrorist organization that toppled the barriers of nationality and religious sect. These widely diverse members united against one common enemy— the United States of America.

THE ROAD TO 9/11

The war with Afghanistan crippled the Soviet Union. In 1991, the Soviet regime fell, finally bringing an end to the Cold War. The United States hoped that terrorism would disintegrate without the support of its communist strong arm, so Congress reduced the amount of money spent on U.S. defense. Meanwhile, though, a new type of terrorist was taking shape in the Middle East. Islamic extremists with the same beliefs and often direct links to Osama bin Laden formed alliances. Following attacks on U.S. forces in Yemen and Somalia, foreign terrorists took their first stab at the American homeland. On February 26, 1993, plotters set off a bomb in the underground parking lot below the north tower of the World Trade Center in New York City. Their plan was to bring the twin towers crashing down, but it failed. Still, six people were killed and more than 1,000 were wounded. Just months later, the police arrested eight extremists who were plotting a "Day of Terror" in which they would blow up landmarks around New York City. Unfortunately, at the time, the authorities did not grasp that these incidents were a preview of attacks to come.

After these scares, funding for national security began to rise. Then, two events occurred in 1995 that forced the government to face the new forms that terrorism could take. One of these attacks did not happen on U.S. soil; the second did. In the 1980s, a superstitious and mystic man named Asahara Shoko began a religious cult in Japan. Although he openly preached hatred of America and the coming of the end of the world, the United States paid little attention to the cult, called Aum Shinrikyo. On March 20, 1995, members of the cult released sarin gas into the Tokyo subway system, killing 12 commuters and sickening 5,000 others. The cult intended to murder a vast number of people, but the chemical agent its members used was of poor quality and the terrorists made mistakes in releasing it.

Only a month later, another terrorist attack rocked the lives of U.S. citizens. On the morning of April 19, Timothy McVeigh—part of an anti-government militia movement— parked a rented Ryder truck in front of the Alfred P. Murrah Federal Building in Oklahoma City, Oklahoma. The truck was loaded with 5,000 pounds (2,268 kilograms) of explosives. Shortly after 9:00 A.M., a massive explosion shook the ground and destroyed the entire north side of the building. The blast killed 168 people, including 19 children who were attending a day-care center there. More than 800 others were injured. Until September 11, 2001, the Oklahoma City bombing was the worst act of terrorism on U.S. soil (the bombing of Pan Am Flight 103 stood as the worst against the United States).

The Alfred P. Murrah Federal Building in downtown Oklahoma City is in ruins after an explosion on April 19, 1995. The blast, set off by anti-government extremist Timothy McVeigh, killed 168 people. Until the attacks of September 11, 2001, the Oklahoma City bombing was the worst terrorist act on U.S. soil.

Americans were stunned. They were unaccustomed to witnessing such a vicious terrorist attack right in the United States. On June 21, 1995, President Bill Clinton issued Presidential Decision Directive 39, which gave the highest priority to developing effective ways to detect, prevent, defeat, and manage the consequences of nuclear, biological, or chemical weapons used by terrorists. Federal spending for security against weapons of mass destruction (WMD) skyrocketed from next to nothing in 1995 to $1.5 billion in 2000.

Abroad, terrorist attacks continued to mount. In 1996, a truck bomb tore apart the Khobar Towers, a U.S. military complex in Dhahran, Saudi Arabia, killing 19 Americans and wounding hundreds. President Clinton vowed to punish "the coward who committed this murderous act," but the terrorists responsible have yet to be punished. Clinton pulled American soldiers out of the Khobar Towers and relocated them to a remote area of Saudi Arabia. Even after the 1993 World Trade Center attack and the Oklahoma City bombing, the terrorist threat still seemed so far away from home.

A NEW BREED OF TERRORIST

On a quiet day in September, a group of highly trained terrorists unleashed a plot to hijack four airliners filled with passengers headed to U.S. destinations. The hijackers were members of an internationally feared terrorist group with a fanatical loyalty to their leader, nicknamed the "Master." At the end of their mission, the planes were destroyed in a fiery explosion, captured by the media. This event, however, happened in 1970, not 2001. The terrorist group was the Popular Front for the Liberation of Palestine, not al Qaeda. And before blowing up the jets, these terrorists evacuated all the prisoners. Their intent was not mass murder. Instead, they wanted the release of imprisoned terrorists and fantastic publicity.

There is a mind-numbing similarity between the 1970 hijackings and the 9/11 attacks. The outcomes, though, reveal a shocking change in terrorist agendas. In 1970, terrorists blew up planes. Three decades later, hijackers not only sent the jets to a fiery grave, but also took the passengers, people on the ground, and themselves with them.

In the late 1990s, al Qaeda and its supporters continued attacks overseas, targeting U.S. embassies and military bases. In 1998, bin Laden swore to drive the United States from the Middle East. President Clinton's administration tried diplomatic missions, economic sanctions, covert operations, and even a missile attack against bin Laden and his followers. But U.S. strategies were created to deal with state-sponsored terrorists. During the Clinton administration and the early Bush administration, the focus remained on the threat in other countries, not at home.

What the U.S. government failed to recognize was that modern extremists were a whole new breed of terrorists. Asahara Shoko was not sponsored by a state. The terrorists did not come from the tents of a refugee camp, but from fine middle-class homes. Unlike Puerto Rican nationalists or communists, they did not have specific political goals but rather a broad, global vision for the future. For example, Palestinian terrorists of the 1960s and 1970s used hostage exchanges to gain tactical advantages against Israel. Communist groups were focused on "freeing" their nations from capitalism. Modern terrorists, though, play by a new set of rules. Instead of perpetrating targeted acts of violence, they choose bold attempts at mass death and destruction toward any government that opposes their Islamic beliefs.

Al Qaeda's goals were to banish American-friendly governments and U.S. influence in Saudi Arabia, Egypt, and other Arab states, as well as destroy the state of Israel. As part of this plan, al Qaeda strove to crush the will of the United States and its Western allies. It also sought to destroy America's capability to resist extremist governments. Al Qaeda did not claim to represent one province, country, region, or class. Instead, it called on the more than one billion Muslims throughout the world. Although it is primarily made up of Sunni Muslims, al Qaeda also gained the support of Shiite extremists. Earlier terrorist groups may have used wide-ranging appeals like communism, racism, and pan-Arabism, but no group has succeeded in creating a unified call to arms like al Qaeda.

FOR ALLAH

Radical terrorist groups like al Qaeda and their sponsors are certainly the most potent terrorist threat to the United States. These groups operate under a powerful ideology—Islamic extremism, a radical version of the Muslim faith.

More than one billion people from dozens of countries are Muslim. Contrary to popular belief, most of these people are not Arabs. They live in countries around the globe, including Indonesia, Pakistan, India, Turkey, Egypt, Nigeria, and Morocco, even the United States and China. Only a small fraction of Muslims support terrorism.

Terrorists have twisted Islam's principles. Islam hails that "there is no god but Allah, and Muhammad is his Prophet." In Arabic, Islam means "submission." Someone who submits to Allah is Muslim. Muslims believe that a merchant from Saudi Arabia named Muhammad, who lived from 570 to 632, received revelations from God. These words that came to Muhammad are written in the Qur'an—Islam's holy scripture, much like Christianity's Holy Bible. According to Islam, Muhammad was the final prophet. Although Muslims do believe that biblical figures like Abraham, Moses, and Jesus all had revelations from God, the Islamic faith does not accept that Christ is God. Similar to Jews and Christians, however, Muslims believe in eternal life, heaven and hell, and Judgment Day.

About 30 years after Muhammad died, a civil war divided Muslims into sects. The two sects most prominent today are the Sunni and the Shiite. Sunnis make up the majority of the population of the Middle East countries and Indonesia, plus much of the Muslim population in other nations. Osama bin Laden and most al Qaeda members are Sunni. Sunnis are followers of the *sunna* (practice) of the prophet Muhammad. The second largest group is the Shiite (or Shi-a) Muslims. They believe that Ali—the son-in-law of Muhammad—was the first of 12 imams appointed by God to succeed Muhammad as leader of the Muslims. Iran is almost entirely Shiite, and much of Iraq is as well, even though members of the Sunni minority basically ruled Iraq under Saddam Hussein's regime. Many Shiites also live in Pakistan and Turkey.

Muslims live by a strict set of codes and rules. They are not allowed to eat pork or drink alcohol. Leaders can make *fatwas*—or religious orders—requiring someone to perform a certain act. The Islamic faith also teaches *jihad*, which for most means striving for the victory of God's (Allah's) word in a person's own life or in the community. To a few, it represents a holy war against infidels, or nonbelievers. Both fatwa and jihad have been twisted by extremists, who use them to justify terrorism, even though many Islamic leaders disagree with such acts. Islamic radicals are often called "Jihadists," because they are committed to waging holy war against Western countries. Extremists claim they are fighting a defensive jihad against the United States in a war for religious control of the world— a war that began 1,000 years ago with the Crusades.

A common tool of Islamic militants is the suicide attack. In a suicide attack, terrorists are willing to kill themselves in order for the strike to succeed. As gory as it seems, for terrorists, suicide missions have tactical advantages. The bomber can deliver the explosive directly to the heart of the target, increasing the chances of a successful mission. There is no need for an escape plan and no risk of capture—therefore, no worry that the group's secrets

WEAPONS OF MASS DESTRUCTION

★ ★ ★ ★ ★

The term *weapons of mass destruction* (WMD) is often uttered in the world of national security. WMDs generally include nuclear, biological, chemical, and radiological weapons. The Department of Homeland Security and the U.S. government go to painstaking efforts to make sure that WMDs stay out of the hands of terrorists.

The most commonly discussed WMD are nuclear weapons. Currently, eight countries are known to have nuclear weapons–the United States, China, Russia, France, India, Israel, Pakistan, and Great Britain. In October 2006, North Korea tested a nuclear weapon. A nuclear weapon kills through blast, heat, and nuclear radiation. An explosion of 2.5 kilotons (equal to the explosive energy of 2,500 tons of TNT) will bring immediate death to anyone within a range of one kilometer, or about six-tenths of a mile.

Radiological weapons, or dirty bombs, rely on radiation rather than the explosion to kill. Radiation destroys or damages cells within the body. High doses of radiation will kill or seriously weaken people. Lower doses can create both short-term and long-term effects. Exposure to radiation will weaken the immune system, making a person more susceptible to illness and disease. Years later, exposure can cause people to develop various types of cancer.

might be told. In the case of the 9/11 attacks, the terrorists delivered a level of death and destruction that was unattainable by any other means. There is also a psychological impact—it magnifies the dedication and the power of terrorists and the vulnerability of the victims.

Chemical weapons can inflict a variety of wounds—from mild irritation to permanent injury and even death. For example, a light dose of mustard gas will cause painful skin blisters and eye and lung irritation over a period of a few hours. On the other hand, someone who inhales 100 milligrams of sarin—a deadly nerve gas—for one minute has a 50 percent chance of dying within just 15 minutes.

A stranger and even more frightening form of WMD is the biological weapon. Biological weapons use living microorganisms, like bacteria, fungi, and viruses, that act as poisons and cause deadly infections. A gram or less of many biological weapons can kill thousands. The most effective form of delivery is by aerosol sprayers, like crop dusters or the air tankers used to fight forest fires. Biological weapons can also be built into a bomb, which will destroy some of the organisms when it explodes. Some biological agents can be sprinkled on sidewalks or dusted on letters. Once contracted, infectious-disease forms of biological weapons can spread from person to person, multiplying the death toll by thousands. Some people worry that smallpox, a once-eradicated disease, might be re-released into the population as a WMD.

Most Islamic scholars and clerics condemn the use of suicide attacks, but the militant groups have corrupted the religion as justification for their methods. They see the attacks as self-sacrifice, or martyrdom, for the cause of jihad. *Istishad* is an Arabic religious term that means "to give one's life for Allah." To the terrorists, to die in this way is acceptable and honorable. In the terrifying tape of Flight 93's final moments, the hijackers cry out in praise of Allah.

A CHILLING CLOSE CALL

On a brisk afternoon in December 1999, a green Chrysler sedan rolled off the ferry sailing from Vancouver Island in Canada to Port Angeles, Washington. A customs agent walked up to the vehicle and asked the driver for his paperwork. She noticed that the young man was unusually fidgety and seemed nervous. After further questioning, the car was searched. In the trunk, the police found 88 pounds (40 kilograms) of explosives and detonators. The man later confessed to authorities that he was planning to use the explosives to bomb Los Angeles International Airport as part of an al Qaeda millennium terrorist plot. He chose the Los Angeles airport because it represented a political and economic symbol of the United States. The young terrorist insisted that he had conceived the plot by himself, although al Qaeda knew about his plans and supplied some support. Despite this chilling close call, the U.S. government still did not have much of an appetite for homeland security. Americans sat unprepared for what would happen next.

4

COWARDLY ACTS

Just before 8:00 in the morning on September 11, 2001, passengers boarded American Airlines Flight 11 and United Airlines Flight 175 at Logan International Airport in Boston. Minutes after the planes took off, American Airlines Flight 77 departed from Washington Dulles International Airport outside the nation's capital. All three flights were bound for Los Angeles, California. Because of a 40-minute delay, United Airlines Flight 93, headed for San Francisco, California, did not take off from Newark International Airport in New Jersey until 8:42. Hijackers took control of all four planes soon after takeoff. Containing nearly 24,000 gallons (91,000 liters) of jet fuel, each aircraft became a flying bomb.

At 8:46 A.M., American Airlines Flight 11 crashed between floors 94 and 98 in the north tower of the World Trade Center, traveling around 490 miles per hour. The

Smoke, flames, and debris erupted from the south tower of the World Trade Center just after it was struck by United Airlines Flight 175 on September 11, 2001. American Airlines Flight 11 had crashed into the north tower *(at right)* sixteen and a half minutes earlier.

impact sent a massive shockwave down to the ground and up again. Within seconds, the plane burst into flames. Sixteen and a half minutes later, media crews and passersby on the ground watched in shock as United Airlines Flight 175 flew into the south tower, between floors 78 and 84. Any thoughts that the first crash was an accident quickly evaporated. These acts could only mean one thing—terrorism.

The people trapped above the floors of impact were in a desperate situation. The smoke and scalding heat from the fire were unbearable. About 200 people jumped to their deaths from the burning towers, landing on streets and rooftops hundreds of feet below. Some workers made their way to the towers' rooftops in hopes of being rescued by helicopters. The thick smoke and intense heat, though, prevented any helicopters from landing.

Meanwhile, people around the world stood mesmerized in front of television sets. Reports that the planes had been hijacked spilled out on television and radio programs. Then, another horror was revealed. American Airlines Flight 77 had spiraled into the western side of the Pentagon in Washington, D.C., igniting into a violent fire. The country was under attack. Federal authorities quickly shut down all U.S. airspace, banning all takeoffs and ordering all planes in flight to land at the nearest airport. A little more than an hour after the first jet plunged into the World Trade Center, the south tower collapsed. On the ground, people ran for cover as glass, concrete, and metal rained down on them. A vast TV audience watched in astonishment as the building crumbled in a billowing cloud of dust.

Only minutes later, United Airlines Flight 93 crashed in a field southeast of Pittsburgh, Pennsylvania. Later, sources revealed that passengers talking on cell phones had learned about the World Trade Center and Pentagon attacks. Upon hearing this news, some passengers decided to resist the hijackers. This act of bravery caused

Three rescue workers are seen walking from the crash site at the Pentagon, which had been hit by American Airlines Flight 77. Soon after the Pentagon was struck, federal authorities shut down U.S. airspace, banning all takeoffs and requiring flights in progress to land at the closest airport.

Two men assisted an injured woman along a street in Lower Manhattan that was littered with paper and ash after the collapse of the World Trade Center towers on September 11, 2001.

the plane to crash before it reached its intended target. Twenty minutes later, the north tower of the World Trade Center fell from the top down, as if it were being peeled apart. In less than two hours, nearly 3,000 people had died. It was one of the most appalling and destructive attacks in history.

That evening, President George W. Bush addressed the nation. He vowed that the United States would hunt down and punish those responsible for these "cowardly acts." Terrorist attacks are considered cowardly because the people who carry them out hide their faces and often plan to commit suicide in the attack. "Terrorist attacks can shake the foundations of our biggest buildings, but they cannot touch the foundation of America," Bush said. "These acts shatter steel, but they cannot dent the steel of American resolve." At home and around the world, the U.S. military was put on high alert, and leaders promised to do whatever was necessary to protect the United States.

WHAT HAPPENED?

The 19 hijackers came from Saudi Arabia, Lebanon, Egypt, and the United Arab Emirates. Other people involved in the plot were from France, Germany, Kuwait, and Yemen. Of course, al Qaeda members are found all around the world. Al Qaeda operations have been linked to people from Somalia, Eritrea, Kenya, Pakistan, Bosnia, Algeria, Croatia, the United States, the Philippines, and many other countries. Still, with FBI intelligence and a strong military defense system, many Americans believed that the United States should have been able to derail this plot. As the smoke and dust cleared, many people stood wide-eyed and shocked, wondering, "What just happened?"

Unveiling a terrorist is no small task. From 1996 to 2000, al Qaeda trained up to 20,000 terrorists in Afghan camps. Not only were they dedicated to their cause, they had been expertly trained on how to act. Most of the hijackers did not have terrorist records, which helped them escape

President George W. Bush addressed the nation from the Oval Office of the White House on September 11, 2001. Bush vowed that the United States would hunt down those responsible for the "cowardly acts" of terrorism.

the attention of U.S. authorities. The al Qaeda manual instructed them to stay clean-shaven and abandon traditional Muslim clothing. Their objective was to blend in with other Americans. They were schooled in Western culture and even shopped at Wal-Mart and ate at Pizza Hut. According to Osama bin Laden, even though the hijackers knew they would be part of a suicide mission, they did not know the details or targets until the operation was well under way. Other than participating in diabolical

THE BUSH DOCTRINE

★ ★ ★ ★ ★

On September 20, 2001, President George W. Bush announced an aggressive offensive against global terrorism. "Every nation in every region now has a decision to make," Bush declared in his speech to Congress. "Either you are with us, or you are with the terrorists. From this day forward, any nation that continues to harbor or support terrorism will be regarded by the United States as a hostile regime." The policy behind those words would come to be known as the Bush Doctrine. Three main threats are singled out: 1) terrorist organizations with a global reach, like al Qaeda; 2) weak or unstable countries that harbor, or hide and protect, terrorists from other countries and regions; and 3) "rogue" states that might help terrorists or perpetrate their own terrorist acts.

One country known to harbor terrorists was Afghanistan, the suspected home of Osama bin Laden. After 9/11, the United States ordered Afghanistan's Taliban rulers to hand over bin Laden. When they repeatedly refused, they were considered a hostile regime. On October 7, 2001, the United States and coalition of countries attacked Afghanistan with air raids and ground forces. Kabul—Afghanistan's capital—fell to U.S. forces on November 13. Many key Taliban and al Qaeda leaders, including bin Laden, however, escaped capture.

acts, modern terrorists appear to have otherwise normal lives. All of these factors made the plot difficult for intelligence to expose.

Al Qaeda attacks take years to plan. The plot for the 9/11 mission began to take shape in the mid-1990s. The ability of these terrorists to envision the event, plan such

The Bush Doctrine was formalized in a document, *The National Security Strategy of the United States of America*. The policy places emphasis on a commitment to promote democracy and freedom in all regions and on military pre-emption, or the idea of cutting off potential aggressors before they can strike the United States.

The doctrine has sparked controversy across the nation and around the world. Because terrorism can vary so widely, there is no clear enemy to fight. Also, battling terrorists does not resemble a traditional war, which has a clear beginning, a definite end, and ways to measure success, usually in the form of territory gained and enemy forces destroyed. In addition, many people thought that other nations might see the U.S. plan as "empire-building"—a chance to expand power rather than increase global security. Many others, though, supported the president's strategy. They thought the United States had no other choice. The traditional ways of dealing with terrorism had not worked. Maybe it was time to try new tactics. To many, the only solution was to go after the terrorists, while preparing the nation for the possibility of another attack. This strategy would grow to include the liberation of Iraq.

an intricate operation, and successfully seize four aircraft and guide three of them into their intended targets proved that a whole new level of terrorist capability was on the rise. Still, in 2000 and 2001, there were a variety of leads and warnings. Just a month before the attack, FBI agents arrested an al Qaeda member who was later suspected of having connections to the attack. But the U.S. homeland security system failed to detect plans for a massive terrorist strike. The country's failure stemmed from an array of problems, including unorganized government strategies, inadequate resources, poor technology, and an FBI whose mindset was stuck on investigating terrorists instead of preventing terrorist attacks. Another roadblock was the communication and cooperation barriers between intelligence and criminal agents. For example, when an FBI agent in New York asked for help from criminal agents to track down two al Qaeda members—who later participated in the 9/11 attacks—he was turned away because of the "wall" between prosecution and intelligence.

After the fact, it did little good to stand around pointing fingers of blame. One fact, however, was certain: Drastic changes needed to be made to protect the United States. What followed was the most dramatic reorganization of the federal government in more than 50 years.

5

Counterterrorism:
The Modern
Homeland Security

The 9/11 attacks changed the United States forever and altered homeland security like nothing before had. As exhausted rescue workers dug through the smoking rubble of the World Trade Center, officials in the Bush administration feverishly mapped out a response to history's most heinous terrorist acts. Immediately after the attacks, authorities grounded all civilian aircraft and closed key government offices and monuments, like the United Nations and the U.S. Capitol. The military deployed fighter jets to fly over major cities in case of another attempt to attack. And intelligence agencies launched a dragnet operation to flush out anyone who was suspected of having terrorist links.

57

Within the government, obvious changes needed to be made to the homeland security system. For years, homeland security had been handled the same way. The 2001 attacks made it painfully obvious that the old-fashioned strategies were insufficient to deal with modern terrorism. A new approach was promoted—counterterrorism, action intended to counteract or suppress terrorism. The Bush administration began to revamp intelligence procedures, as well as the FBI and other federal agencies. The administration created the White House Office of Homeland Security and drafted a national homeland security strategy, which was released in July 2002. *The National Strategy for Homeland Security* laid out three objectives: preventing an attack, reducing vulnerability to an attack, and minimizing damage if an attack occurred. In addition, the report created a definition for a terrorist act: any premeditated, unlawful act that endangers human life or the public welfare and is intended to intimidate or coerce citizens or governments.

The Office of Homeland Security also made plans to establish a special military unit to defend North America and proposed the idea of a federal homeland security department. About a year later, in October 2002, the U.S. Northern Command (NORTHCOM) was established. Before 9/11, no single military command was responsible for defending the United States. NORTHCOM guards the land, air, and sea in and around North America. The following month, the Homeland Security Act of 2002 combined 22 federal agencies and more than 180,000 employees into a single department that would monitor immigration enforcement, border and transportation security, emergency preparedness and response, and science and technology for homeland security. The Department of Homeland Security also took control of the Transportation Security Administration, which had been created to screen commercial airline passengers and cargo, as well as secure railways and public transit systems. Immediately after the 9/11 strikes, the government recruited, trained, and deployed 45,000 federal security screeners to airports across the country.

Still, there were more improvements being made. Congress passed aggressive legislation to strengthen law enforcement at the federal, state, and local levels. The Aviation and Transportation Security Act, passed in November 2001, was the act that established the Transportation Security Administration. The Maritime Transportation Security Act imposed new requirements for the security of ports and for shipping. To help tag potential terrorists as they entered the country, visitors to the United States were required to provide more information through the Enhanced Border Security and Visa Entry Reform Act.

Soon after the 9/11 attacks, another threat jolted Americans. Letters dusted with anthrax bacteria arrived at the offices of various media outlets, including NBC and *The New York Post* in New York City and the *National Enquirer* in Florida. In early October, some U.S. senators also received tainted letters at their offices in Washington, D.C. One letter read:

09-11-01

YOU CAN NOT STOP US.
WE HAVE THIS ANTRAX.
YOU DIE NOW.
ARE YOU AFRAID?
DEATH TO AMERICA.
DEATH TO ISRAEL.
ALLAH IS GREAT.

In early October 2001, FBI agents investigated the discovery of
anthrax at the Florida offices of American Media Inc., publishers of
the *National Enquirer*. Anthrax was also sent to the offices of NBC,
The New York Post, and some U.S. senators. Five people died, and
at least 17 others became ill.

But workers in the media and senators and their staff members were not the only people who were exposed. Postal workers, as well as a woman in Connecticut, contracted inhalation anthrax from spores that leaked out of the letters. In the end, five people died of anthrax infection and at least 17 others became sick. The poisonings struck new fear in the minds of Americans—that of a dangerous biological or chemical threat. In response, Congress passed the Public Health Security and Bioterrorism Preparedness and Response Act to add safety measures to protect the food and drug supply. The anthrax attacks also ignited a push for an increased defense against weapons of mass destruction.

The most significant and controversial antiterrorism law passed by Congress was the Uniting and Strengthening America by Providing Appropriate Tools Required to Intercept and Obstruct Terrorism (USA PATRIOT) Act. This piece of legislation created new crimes, greater penalties, and fresh procedures to use against terrorists at home and around the world. Under the Patriot Act, federal agencies received increased powers to monitor and track suspected terrorists. For example, previous laws only allowed law enforcement officials to install pen registers—devices that record telephone numbers dialed from a suspect's home— and trap and trace devices, which record the numbers of incoming calls. The new law gives agents the authority to monitor a suspect's Internet use, including the tracking of e-mails and Internet activity. Also, in special cases, the Patriot Act gives agents the right to conduct secret searches on suspects instead of requiring them to get a warrant first.

Some people thought that the legislation went too far and that Americans were in danger of having their civil liberties infringed. The law, though, did help the U.S. war on terrorism in four critical areas. First, the new law encouraged intelligence and law enforcement agencies to share information during investigations, knocking down the "wall" that bungled investigations before 9/11. It authorized the use of more law enforcement tools in pursuing terrorists, including technology and other

Demonstrators who opposed the Patriot Act gathered in September 2003 in Durham, North Carolina, across from a hotel where John Ashcroft, then the U.S. attorney general, was speaking. Opponents of the Patriot Act said that it infringed upon the civil rights of Americans.

resources already used in investigations of other serious crimes, like drug smuggling. In addition, the Patriot Act allowed agents to use new technology like cell phones and the Internet to track and monitor terrorists. Finally, judicial and congressional leaders were put in charge of overseeing all of the new authorities created by the legislation. Driven by 9/11, these changes laid the first stones in the foundation for a modern system of homeland security.

A NATION ON HIGH ALERT

Until 9/11, the FBI was more concerned about prosecuting terrorists who had been caught than actively destroying terrorist networks. After the attacks, FBI agents dedicated themselves to preventing terrorism. The most important key to stopping terrorism was united cooperation. Everyone would have to work together to break apart terrorist networks—from the FBI and the CIA to state law enforcement to local police officers to everyday citizens. Everyone in the nation would have to be on high alert, pay attention, and communicate with one another.

Two new organizations were created to aid communications between federal agencies and state and local law enforcement officials. Located at the CIA Headquarters just outside Washington, D.C., the Terrorism Threat Integration Center handles all terrorist-related intelligence, both foreign and domestic. Agents from the FBI, CIA, Department of Defense, Department of Homeland Security, and other intelligence agencies get together and discuss current developments in the war on terrorism. At the second organization, the Terrorist Screening Center, officers collect all terrorist watch lists and input them into a single database. Federal, state, and local authorities have around-the-clock access to these lists.

On September 11, state and local governments received a serious lesson on the role they play in homeland

ALERTING THE NATION

In March 2002, the federal government established the color-coded Homeland Security Advisory System. Each color of the system represents a level of "threat conditions," and state and local authorities must follow the security measure under each code.

Low Threat Condition–Green: This condition is declared when there is a low risk of terrorist attacks. Under the green alert, agencies should continue to watch for vulnerabilities and maintain their security systems.

Guarded Threat Condition–Blue: The blue alert goes into effect when there is a general risk of terrorism. Besides taking the protective measures of the green alert, federal agencies should test communication systems with emergency response and command locations, as well as review and update emergency response procedures. Agencies should also give the public any information that may strengthen security.

Elevated Threat Condition–Yellow: Under a yellow alert, there is a substantial risk of terrorist attacks. In addition to taking the green and blue measures, federal departments and agencies should insecurity. Hundreds of New York City firefighters, police officers, and other first responders died as the twin towers collapsed. Local agencies that responded to the crash at the Pentagon also played a key role in handling the catastrophe. Before 9/11, emergency response teams were trained on what to do in case of a natural disaster or human-made calamities like arson or accidental chemical

crease surveillance of critical locations. Emergency plans should also be coordinated with nearby jurisdictions.

High Threat Condition–Orange: If there is a high risk of terrorism, the nation is put on orange alert. Law enforcement should coordinate necessary security plans with federal, state, and local agencies, as well as with the National Guard and other armed forces. Officers should take special security precautions at public events, and even consider postponing or canceling them. Highly threatened facilities should be restricted to essential personnel only.

Severe Threat Condition–Red: The red threat alerts the country of a severe risk of terrorist attack. All previous color alerts should be implemented. Emergency response teams and other specially trained response personnel should be on standby and ready to move in case of an attack. Law enforcement officials are required to closely monitor transportation systems and, if necessary, restrict travel. All public and government facilities must be closed until further notice.

For the current threat condition, log on to the Department of Homeland Security's Web site at www.dhs.gov.

Tom Ridge, the first director of the Office of Homeland Security, outlined the new color-coded Homeland Security Advisory System during a news conference in March 2002. The system is used to relay information about the risks of terrorist acts to the American people.

spills. Across the country, as state and local governments watched the events unfold, they began to take a harder look at their own emergency response procedures.

Americans are governed by thousands of state and local jurisdictions. These jurisdictions create and carry out most emergency plans. They also direct the police, firefighters, and National Guard troops on the frontlines of homeland security. Until 9/11, most communities invested time and money toward improving security against common crimes. For some state and local governments, these priorities changed after the terrorist attacks. State officials in New Jersey created their own counterterrorism office to prevent and respond to a possible terrorist attack. In New York, the governor proposed expanding the state's investigations for counterterrorism, and New York City alone has spent more than $200 million a year on counterterrorism programs.

Of course, not all communities responded the same way. Many factors contributed to how states and cities reacted to 9/11. Metropolises with potential terrorist targets were eager to strengthen homeland security policies. Smaller cities and rural communities were less likely to increase spending for counterterrorism measures. Still, in total, more than 1,200 state and local legislative acts were passed in the wake of 9/11. The federal government also provided billions of dollars in grants to state and local homeland security agencies.

6

PROTECTING
AMERICA

The Homeland Security Act of 2002, signed on November 25, created the Department of Homeland Security (DHS). The primary purpose of the DHS was to unify all agencies responsible for homeland security and to help improve the efficiency of the agencies. Essentially, the DHS ensures U.S. safety and security in hundreds of ways, addressing potential threats to the nation—both present and future. The DHS is a national mission, connecting more than 87,000 government jurisdictions at the federal, state, and local levels. The DHS officially began to operate on March 1, 2003.

Currently, the Department of Homeland Security is the third-largest cabinet department in the federal government, after the Department of Defense and the Department of Veterans Affairs. It employs about 184,000 people. While the Department of Defense handles *military* actions overseas, the DHS works in the civilian arena to protect the United States within, at, and outside its borders. Traditionally, homeland security functions are dispersed among dozens of federal agencies and thousands of first-responder units across the United States. The DHS streamlines all federal actions into one interconnected unit. It sets one point of contact for state and local groups. In the end, the aim of the department is to create a better prepared and safer America.

When creating the DHS, the vision was to preserve the nation's freedoms and to protect the country. Its mission statement reinforces this vision. "We will lead the unified national effort to secure America. We will prevent and deter terrorist attacks and protect against and respond to threats and hazards to the nation. We will ensure safe and secure borders, welcome lawful immigrants and visitors, and promote the free-flow of commerce." As stated in the department's strategic plan, the core values upon which the DHS was formed are integrity—service before self; vigilance—guarding America; and respect—honoring its partners.

The bulk of the DHS was created from 22 existing federal agencies. It combines much of the executive branch of government, including the Federal Emergency Management Agency (FEMA), the former U.S. Customs Service, and the Transportation Security Administration. These agencies are separated into four main directorates, or branches, of the department—Border and Transportation Security, Emergency Preparedness and Response, Science and Technology, and Information Analysis and Infrastructure Protection. A fifth directorate focuses on management issues. The former Immigration and Naturalization Service—now the Citizenship and Immigration Services—the U.S. Coast Guard, and the U.S. Secret Service are also part of the Department of Homeland Security but exist as distinct entities. Much responsibility for homeland security, however, still falls outside of the department, with the Federal Bureau of Investigation and the Central Intelligence Agency, which operate independent of the DHS.

STRONG BORDERS AND SAFER SKIES

The United States has 5,525 miles (8,892 kilometers) of border with Canada and nearly 2,000 miles (3,220 kilometers) with Mexico, not to mention 95,000 miles (152,900 kilometers) of shoreline. The country's many airports, seaports, and waterways provide hundreds of gateways for illegal goods and dangerous people. These problems include illegal drugs, weapons, smuggled goods, biological agents, and weapons of mass destruction, as well as the people who tote them—smugglers, drug dealers, criminals, and terrorists. Adequate security and control of U.S. borders is essential in protecting the country. From the beginning, increasing border security was a prime focus of the Department of Homeland Security. The DHS has combined the various agencies involved in the safety, security, and control of borders under the Border and Transportation Security directorate.

After 9/11, the U.S. government's immediate response was to tighten border inspections and toughen the policies on border crossings. Today, there are more Border Patrol agents in the San Diego sector alone than there were along the entire 2,000-mile border with Mexico only two decades ago. For years, the United States had the luxury of ignoring the northern border. Before 9/11, the Canadian border,

A Border Patrol agent climbed out of a tunnel discovered in September 2006 in a house in Calexico, California. The tunnel led to a house in Mexico and was used to smuggle drugs and illegal immigrants. By the end of 2008, the government plans to have trained 6,000 new Border Patrol agents.

which has been called "the world's longest undefended border," was barely policed. The northern Border Patrol employed a mere 334 agents compared with the more than 9,000 agents at the Mexican border. On September 11, 2001, there were as many border agents in Brownsville, Texas, as there were on the entire U.S.-Canadian border. The Patriot Act tripled the number of agents deployed to the northern border, and National Guard troops also help with patrols and inspections at border posts. By the end of 2008, the U.S. Border Patrol Academy of U.S. Customs and Border Protection plans to have trained 6,000 new agents to patrol the nation's borders.

Still, keeping the borders safe is a daunting task. Each year, about 300 million people, 90 million cars, and 4.3 million trucks cross into the United States from Mexico. Before the 9/11 attacks, the U.S. Border Patrol mainly focused on intercepting illegal drugs and migrants. Agents basically use the same methods for counterterrorism. While border control successes are notable—thousands of pounds of cocaine and more than a million pounds of marijuana are seized each year—multi-ton shipments of drugs and thousands of illegal migrants still slip across the border. The chance of deterring a few bombs or terrorists is unlikely. In the north, thousands of miles of border are practically wide open. Northern Border Patrol agents face many of the same troubles as those at the southern border. Although the increased security helps make Americans feel safer, it may do more to delay travel, aggravate tourists, and burden trade than keep terrorists out.

The U.S. Coast Guard faces many of the same dilemmas as the Border Patrol. The focus before 9/11 was also on drugs and migrants—only 1 to 2 percent of its time and effort was devoted to detecting possible terrorists. Now, the Coast Guard spends more than 50 percent of its energy on counterterrorism measures, thanks to major increases in federal funding for the programs. In 2003, border security received a $2 billion boost in its budget, the largest budget increase in Coast Guard history.

Because commercial airlines were used in the 2001 attacks, the Office of Homeland Security immediately placed U.S. airports under the spotlight. Today, agencies within the Department of Homeland Security are responsible for keeping transportation safe. Almost immediately, the number of law enforcement officers at airports skyrocketed. President George W. Bush asked the nation's governors to station National Guard units at airports around the country. For the first time, many Americans saw armed soldiers patrolling civilian areas. Many people, still shaky about their safety, were relieved to see the guardsmen. For others, the sight made them uneasy. Images of military states flashed before them. They feared what might become of the free United States.

The use of guardsmen, though, was only a temporary solution while the government created more permanent methods of security. Just two months after the terrorist attacks, Congress passed the Aviation and Transportation Security Act, which created the Transportation Security Administration. The agency made the security of the

United States' 429 commercial airports a federal responsibility. Previously, private companies had run security operations.

Heightened security made air travel drastically different for Americans, especially with the intense screening procedures now required. All checked baggage is thoroughly screened. Screeners use numerous methods to test the bags for explosives. One method is the Explosive Detection System, a large device similar to a hospital CT-scan machine. As luggage moves along a conveyor belt, the machine evaluates the contents of the bags. Airports also

An Explosion Detection System *(center foreground)* has been installed near the ticket counters at Little Rock National Airport in Arkansas. Similar to a hospital CT scan, the machine evaluates the contents of airline passengers' luggage for explosives.

use a smaller device called an Explosive Trace Detection machine. Screeners use a chemically treated swab to rub the surface or inside of a traveler's bag. They then place the swabs into the machine, which analyzes the samples for traces of bomb residue.

Travelers also have to pass through stiff screening before boarding a plane. Passengers and their carry-on luggage have to pass through X-ray machines at security checkpoints. Many airports require fliers to remove their shoes for screening, after the "shoe bomber" incident. In December 2001, a British national who was allied with radical Muslim terrorist groups boarded a plane, bound from Paris to Miami, carrying a homemade bomb in his shoe. Flight attendants and passengers managed to grab him before he could light the explosive. The weapons used in the September 11 hijackings were box cutters, so the government expanded the list of items that are not allowed in carry-on luggage. Prohibited items range from the obvious—guns, knives, and explosives—to items that appear harmless at first but could be used as weapons— like pointed-tip scissors, baseball bats, and pool cues. In the past, family and friends could accompany airline passengers to their gates. Now, only people with boarding passes are allowed near the gates.

At times, security officers pick out some passengers for a secondary screening process using a program called the Computer Assisted Passenger Prescreening System, or CAPPS. CAPPS compares flight lists with public and government records for any terrorist links to passengers.

On 9/11, CAPPS tagged half of the hijackers as potential threats. The officers, though, only gave a more thorough screening to their luggage, which contained no weapons. From time to time, CAPPS can cause problems for law-abiding citizens.

The chance always exists that someone, like the "shoe bomber," might get past the heavy screening. So the government implemented a variety of changes to protect the cockpit once the plane was in the air. Before the terrorist attacks, most cockpit doors were flimsy and could not be locked. The first improvement made to planes was stronger cockpit doors. Immediately after the attacks, existing doors were reinforced with metal bars. By early 2003, all large commercial planes in the United States had lockable, bullet-proof cockpit doors.

The government also increased the number of plainclothes federal air marshals on duty. These armed sky marshals ride on selected flights and can use deadly force on hijackers. Because of the enormous number of flights, a sky marshal cannot be on every plane. The odds, though, are great that a law enforcement officer could be on any given flight. For security reasons, the government does not reveal the exact number of sky marshals, their identities, or which routes they fly.

Even with these extraordinary security measures, some pilots thought they needed more protection. They lobbied Congress to allow them to carry guns in the cockpit. Those against the idea argued that during a hijacking, the pilot should focus on maintaining control of the plane. Furthermore, opponents worried that a pilot might miss the target and damage flight equipment instead. Under the Transportation Security Administration's Federal Flight Deck Officer program, eligible members of the flight crew are authorized to use firearms to defend against a possible hijacking. These flight deck officers are trained in the use of firearms, the use of force, legal issues, and defensive tactics.

Since the airliners in the September 11 attacks were used as missiles, the Department of Defense gave fighter pilots the authority to shoot down hijacked planes. By sacrificing the lives of those on board, thousands more on the ground might be saved.

EMERGENCY PREPAREDNESS AND RESPONSE

The Homeland Security Act of 2002 established the Emergency Preparedness and Response (EPR) directorate in the Department of Homeland Security. Title V of the act transferred the functions, personnel, resources, and authorities of six existing agencies into the directorate. These agencies were:

1) The Federal Emergency Management Agency, more commonly known as FEMA.

2) The Integrated Hazard Information System, previously under the National Oceanic and Atmospheric Administration of the Department of Commerce.

3) The National Domestic Preparedness Office of the FBI and related jobs of the U.S. attorney general.

4) The Domestic Emergency Support Teams of the Department of Justice and the related tasks of the U.S.
attorney general.

5) The Office of Emergency Preparedness and the related
functions of the secretary of the Department of Health
and Human Services and the Assistant Secretary for
Public Health Emergency Preparedness.

6) The Strategic National Stockpile of the Department
of Health and Human Services, and the related jobs
of the secretary. (In the summer of 2004, overall
responsibility for the Strategic National Stockpile
was returned to the Department of Health and
Human Services.)

A seventh capability—the Nuclear Incident Response
Team—is organized, equipped, and trained by the Department of Energy and the Environmental Protection Agency.
This team is directed by the secretary of the Department
of Homeland Security and operates as a unit of the Emergency Preparedness and Response directorate.

The EPR directorate focuses much energy on ensuring
a quick and efficient response to national emergencies.
Through agencies like FEMA, the EPR works to organize
and stabilize the procedures of first responders across the
country. First responders consist of local police officers,
firefighters, and emergency medical professionals. They
are the country's first line of defense in any terrorist attack
or catastrophe. When properly trained, these individuals
have the greatest potential to save lives and limit the

number of deaths in a disaster. One job of the EPR is to provide disaster-preparedness education programs for communities and citizens, and the directorate plans to expand the number of participants in the Community Emergency Response Team program. The directorate also partners with other federal emergency training institutions to standardize training curriculum and provide a single portal for accessing the programs, including anti-terrorism training programs.

The EPR is responsible for coordinating the National Response Plan. First released in December 2004, the National Response Plan is a framework that guides the federal response efforts after a catastrophe. The implementation of the plan falls under the direct responsibility of FEMA. After failures in dealing with Hurricane Katrina in 2005, the National Response Plan was updated and improved. (FEMA and Hurricane Katrina will be covered in Chapter 7.) The EPR also developed hazard warning systems, including the color-coded Homeland Security Advisory System. This system provides a comprehensive and effective way to relay information about the risk of terrorist acts to federal, state, and local authorities, and to the American people.

Currently across the United States, capabilities of first responders vary widely. Many areas still have little or no capability to respond to a terrorist attack that uses weapons of mass destruction. In time, the ERP directorate hopes to equip every community with the tools to respond to and recover from every kind of disaster.

SECRETARIES OF THE DEPARTMENT OF HOMELAND SECURITY

In its short history, the Department of Homeland Security has had two secretaries: Tom Ridge, who served from the department's formation until February 2005; and Michael Chertoff, Ridge's successor.

President George W. Bush tapped Ridge to be the director of the Office of Homeland Security, which was formed after the 9/11 attacks. Before then, Ridge had been the governor of Pennsylvania since 1995. Ridge graduated from Harvard in 1967 and was drafted into the U.S. Army, serving as an infantry staff sergeant in Vietnam. He earned his law degree after the war and was elected to the House of Representatives in 1982. Ridge was the first enlisted Vietnam combat veteran to serve in Congress.

About the Department of Homeland Security, Ridge said: "We have to be right a billion-plus times a year, meaning we have to make literally hundreds of thousands, if not millions, of decisions every year, or every day, and the terrorists only have to be right once."

When Chertoff was nominated to be secretary of homeland security, he was serving as a U.S. circuit judge for the Third Circuit Court of Appeals. He had also served in the Bush administration as an assistant attorney general for the Criminal Division at the Department of Justice.

"In the days after September the 11th, [Chertoff] helped trace the terrorist attacks to the al Qaeda network. He understood immediately that the strategy on the war on terror is to prevent attacks before they occur," Bush said in announcing Chertoff's nomination.

Chertoff had also served for more than a decade as a federal prosecutor, working on cases of political corruption, organized crime, and corporate fraud.

SCIENCE & TECHNOLOGY AND CYBER-PROTECTION

The Science and Technology (S&T) directorate is the primary research and development branch of the Department of Homeland Security. Agencies within the directorate conduct research on homeland security technologies for federal, state, and local officials. The primary function of the S&T is to provide officials with state-of-the-art technology that will help protect the homeland. Its mission is accomplished through six major goals:

1) Develop and deploy state-of-the-art, high-performance, low-operating-cost systems that prevent, detect, and lessen the consequences of chemical, biological, radiological, nuclear, and explosive attacks.

2) Develop equipment, protocols, and training procedures for response to and recovery from chemical, biological, radiological, nuclear, and explosive attacks.

3) Enhance the technical capabilities of the DHS operations, as well as other federal, state, local, and tribal agencies to fulfill their security-related missions.

4) Develop methods and capabilities to test and assess threats and vulnerabilities, and to prevent technology surprise and anticipate emerging threats.

5) Develop technical standards and establish certified laboratories to evaluate homeland security and emergency responder technologies.

6) Support U.S. leadership in science and technology.

Michael Chertoff *(left)*, the current secretary of the Department of Homeland Security, participated in March 2005 in a U.S. Coast Guard change-of-watch ceremony with Tom Ridge, his predecessor at the department. The ceremony was held at Fort McNair in Washington, D.C.

Most S&T research is managed by the Homeland Security Advanced Research Projects Agency (HSARPA). A common misconception of many is that the HSARPA is like the Department of Defense agency, the Defense Advanced Research Projects Agency (DARPA), whose radical research played an important role in the development of the Internet. Rather, the primary focus of the HSARPA is on short-term capabilities that can be ready for use in six months to two years, not high-risk ventures that might result in extraordinary technologies.

Inside the world of technology, the Information Analysis and Infrastructure Protection directorate fights to keep technologies—like the Internet, telecommunications, and security systems—safe from terrorist predators. Over recent years, the Internet has become one of the nation's greatest communication tools. The IAIP plays "cyber-cop" against any terrorist who tries to infiltrate secret government data.

Sometimes, the people who steal government secrets work for the government themselves. Robert Hanssen was a trusted FBI agent in charge of hunting down foreign spies in the United States. His job included some of the most secret and sensitive work in the agency. In 2001, other FBI agents discovered that *he* was actually a spy for the Soviet Union and then Russia. For more than a decade, he had been stealing secret data from the FBI, including encrypted floppy disks, removable storage devices, and a Palm handheld device.

Cyberterrorism affects the world of computers. Perpetrators commit cyberterrorism by stealing information, corrupting data, covertly taking remote control of computers, or shutting down entire systems. Cyber-attacks can be against a single computer or affect mass numbers of computers by denying access to the Internet. The highest percentage of illegal computer attacks are committed by "insiders" like Hanssen—employees who have easy access to the computers and records they want to steal or corrupt. Just as the Soviet Union used Hanssen, terrorists can use insiders to carry out their destructive missions.

Outside attacks occur less frequently. But some security analysts believe outside attacks could be a greater threat. These strikes occur through the Internet and can originate from anywhere in the world. Almost any state or nonstate group can launch a cyber-attack. Cyber-crimes can be used to supplement or aid other terrorist crimes. For example, high-tech computer systems monitor and control the transfer of electricity and the flow of oil and gas through pipelines. An attack to these systems might trigger power outages, spark explosions, or unleash fuel spills.

Within the IAIP, the National Cyber Security Division works to develop a national cyberspace security response system. The division is responsible for running cyberspace analysis, issuing alerts and warnings, responding to major incidents, and overseeing national recovery efforts. Although modern technology is an incredible asset, it can open up a whole new arena for terrorist attacks.

7

THE TEST

On August 23, 2005, a tropical storm formed over the southeastern Bahamas. Rapidly growing in intensity, it was given a name—Katrina. As the storm moved toward Florida, it escalated to a Category 1 hurricane only two hours before it made landfall just north of Miami during the evening of August 25. (Hurricanes are classified on a scale from 1 to 5, with Category 5 being the most severe storm.) Katrina was the eleventh named storm—and fifth hurricane—of the 2005 Atlantic hurricane season. Katrina weakened over land, but then it passed into the Gulf of Mexico.

There, the hurricane regained its power, bulking up to a whopping Category 5 storm. Katrina became one of the strongest hurricanes on record. On the morning of August 27—two days before Katrina would make landfall in Louisiana—the National Hurricane Center issued a hurricane

Four days after Hurricane Katrina made landfall on the Gulf Coast, many parts of New Orleans remained flooded. Levees that separated Lake Pontchartrain from the city were breached, and 80 percent of New Orleans was flooded. About a quarter-million people were displaced.

watch for southeastern Louisiana, including the New Orleans area. That afternoon, the watch was extended to cover the Mississippi and Alabama coastlines as well. Voluntary and mandatory evacuations were being issued across the Gulf Coast.

By Sunday, August 28, as the strength and size of Katrina became clear, the National Weather Service's New Orleans/Baton Rouge office issued a vivid bulletin, predicting that the New Orleans area would be uninhabitable for weeks after the hurricane. That morning, New

Orleans Mayor Ray Nagin ordered the first-ever mandatory evacuation of the city. The city government also established several refuges of last resort for people who were
unable to leave the city, including the Louisiana Superdome, which could shelter 26,000 people.

President George W. Bush declared a state of emergency for Louisiana on August 27 and for Mississippi and
Alabama the next day, ordering federal aid to complement
state and local relief efforts. Most of the infrastructure,
or basic facilities and services, along the Gulf Coast shut
down ahead of the storm. Katrina would be the first
major test for the Department of Homeland Security and
its Emergency Preparedness and Response directorate.
Many Americans would come to believe that the government failed miserably.

THE STORM STRIKES

The morning of August 29, Hurricane Katrina first made
landfall in southeast Louisiana, kicking up winds of more
than 140 miles per hour (225 kilometers per hour). When
the eye of the hurricane passed east of New Orleans, Katrina had been downgraded to a Category 3 storm; still,
wind gusts of more than 100 miles per hour (160 kilometers per hour) were reported. The hurricane then made its
second landfall on the Mississippi-Louisiana border, with
winds of 125 miles per hour (201 kilometers per hour). For
several hours, rainfall rates exceeded an inch an hour.

In New Orleans, much of which lies below sea level,
storm surges caused breaches in the flood-protection levee

system, flooding 80 percent of the city. Large portions of Biloxi and Gulfport, in Mississippi, were underwater as a result of a 20-to-30-foot (6-to-9-meter) storm surge from the Gulf of Mexico. Further east, a storm surge from Mobile Bay inundated Mobile, Alabama. Across parts of Louisiana, Mississippi, and Alabama, Katrina left catastrophic damage. The hardest-hit communities lost all infrastructure: electricity, water, roads, communications systems, and even basic government operations like law enforcement.

Back in New Orleans, the hurricane and flooding left up to 100,000 people stranded in squalid and flooded conditions. The city had no power, no drinking water, dwindling food supplies, and widespread looting. Rescuers were saving hundreds of people from rooftops. Poor communications, though, delayed state and federal officials from learning where the rescued victims had been taken, slowing supply shipments to those areas. Thousands more were seeking shelter at the Superdome, but conditions there were deteriorating rapidly. Toilets were overflowing, there was little power, and without air-conditioning, the 90-degree heat was stifling. By Wednesday, August 31, buses began to evacuate people from the Superdome. Thousands more were stranded at the convention center in New Orleans, where a convoy of food, water, and medicine did not arrive until four days after the hurricane struck.

In total, Katrina pounded out $125 billion in damages and claimed more than 1,800 lives—making it the deadliest hurricane to hit the United States in more than

People walked along flooded railroad tracks near the Louisiana Superdome in New Orleans. Those who did not or could not evacuate from New Orleans took refuge at the Superdome, but conditions there quickly deteriorated.

75 years. About three-quarters of all the houses in New Orleans were damaged or destroyed. In Mississippi, two-thirds of the homes in the six southernmost counties were severely damaged or destroyed.

Across the country, Americans watched televised images of people in New Orleans and across the Gulf Coast without water, food, or shelter. FEMA came under fire for its slow response and apparent inability to manage, care for, and move those trying to flee the city. The deaths of citizens from thirst, exhaustion, or violence days after the storm fueled the criticism. There were even reports that FEMA, in some instances, turned away fuel and water trucks. On September 12, two weeks after Katrina hit the Gulf Coast, the director of FEMA, Michael Brown, resigned.

FEMA UNDER FIRE

According to the National Response Plan, disaster response and planning is first and foremost a local government responsibility. When the local government exhausts its resources, then the county and state governments step in. After these resources run out, the federal government lends a hand. Well aware of the size and destructiveness of Katrina, many critics feel that FEMA should have been poised for immediate action and was not. Much of the frustration with the disaster response circled around New Orleans. In fact, FEMA had prepositioned disaster-response teams in the Gulf Coast region. And in departing from standard practice, the governors of the three affected states requested, and President Bush issued, emergency declarations before Katrina made landfall. The massive strength of the storm and the enormous number of evacuees, however, were too much.

"Although FEMA and other agencies deployed emergency responders and resources in advance of the storm and supported state efforts to evacuate people and conduct other preparations, most were overwhelmed the first week after landfall," stated a report by the Department of Homeland Security's own inspector general, or internal watchdog, on FEMA's activities in response to Katrina.

And while relief efforts were overwhelmed, in some instances, the response suffered from a failure to understand the effects of the disaster, according to a report on Katrina by the U.S. Senate Committee on Homeland Security and Governmental Affairs. The Senate committee's report indicated that reliable information about levee failures, the extent of flooding, and the thousands of people stranded at the convention center did not reach the White House or DHS Secretary Michael Chertoff in a timely manner.

"DHS was slow to recognize the scope of the disaster or that FEMA had become overwhelmed," the Senate committee's report said. "On the day after landfall, DHS officials were still struggling to determine the 'ground truth' about the extent of the flooding despite the many reports it had received about the catastrophe; key officials did not grasp the need to act on the less-than-complete information that is to be expected in a disaster."

But DHS and FEMA were not the only targets for criticism. With all the alerts and warnings before Katrina made

Within the Department of Homeland Security, under the Emergency Preparedness and Response directorate, the Federal Emergency Management Agency, or FEMA, is responsible for coordinating emergency relief to disasters that occur in the United States. FEMA responds if a disaster overwhelms state and local authorities, often after the governor has declared a state of emergency and requested federal help.

Federal emergency management has existed in one form or another for more than 200 years. The first major disaster in U.S. history was a series of devastating fires in the port city of Portsmouth, New Hampshire. In response, Congress passed the Congressional Act of 1803, which offered financial relief to merchants by waiving duties and tariffs on goods. This law was the first piece of legislation passed by the federal government that provided disaster relief; it set the foundation for future disaster-relief policies.

By 1960, the government had created the Federal Disaster Assistance Administration. This agency oversaw disasters such as a series of hurricanes that occured throughout the 1960s. At this time, many other government agencies also had played roles in disaster-relief services. In some cases, more than 100 agencies might have been jockeying for control over a disaster area.

In 1979, President Jimmy Carter put a new agency—FEMA—in charge of coordinating all disaster-relief efforts at the federal level. One of FEMA's first responses was to the dumping of toxic waste in the Love Canal neighborhood of Niagara Falls, New York. FEMA also responded to the partial core meltdown at the Three Mile Island nuclear power plant in 1979. President Bill Clinton elevated FEMA to cabinet-level status in 1993. In 2003, FEMA became part of the Department of Homeland Security. Today, the agency has more than 2,600 full-time employees.

landfall, some found it baffling that so many people were stranded in New Orleans. Much of this heat fell on the local and state governments, headed by Mayor Nagin and Louisiana Governor Kathleen Blanco. Nagin and Blanco were criticized for failing to implement a suitable evacuation plan. Nagin delayed his emergency evacuation order until 19 hours before Katrina made landfall. By that time, many people could not find any way out of the city.

"The incomplete pre-landfall evacuation led to deaths, thousands of dangerous rescues, and horrible conditions for those who remained," stated the final report issued by the U.S. House of Representatives committee that investigated the preparation for the response to Katrina.

In the mass confusion, it seemed as if the Department of Homeland Security had failed its first real test. Undoubtedly, FEMA had bungled an efficient emergency response through poor communication, mismanagement, and a lack of leadership. Still, thousands of lives were saved through its rescue efforts. The response and aftermath, though, pointed to the need for continued improvements to the nation's state of preparedness on all levels.

The House committee's report stated: "The failure of local, state, and federal governments to respond more effectively to Katrina—which had been predicted in theory for many years, and forecast with startling accuracy for five days—demonstrates that whatever improvements have been made to our capacity to respond to natural or manmade disasters, four and a half years after 9/11, we are still not fully prepared."

More than a week after Hurricane Katrina had struck, a resident living in a tented city in Bay St. Louis, Mississippi, put up a sign criticizing FEMA. The resident had called FEMA four times and was always prompted to leave a message.

A year after Hurricane Katrina, FEMA has shown signs of improvement. According to an article in *The New York Times*, the agency has adopted policies to prevent fraud and wasteful spending, has bolstered its ties with other federal agencies to help with evacuations and emergency medical aid, and has begun using high-tech equipment like a system that tracks supplies headed toward a disaster zone. On the other hand, the article stated, the Department of Homeland Security rated only 27 percent of states and 10 percent of cities it evaluated as prepared to cope with a major catastrophe.

THE FUTURE OF HOMELAND SECURITY

September 11, 2001, was not the first act of terrorism in the United States. It was not the most destructive disaster to hit the nation. However, 9/11 incited in Americans the fear, anger, patriotism, bravery, compassion, and ambition necessary to bring great change inside the federal government and across the country.

Out of the dust of the twin towers rose two far-reaching pieces of legislation—the USA Patriot Act and the Homeland Security Act. The Patriot Act gave the U.S. attorney general and the Department of Justice expanded law enforcement authority for the purpose of fighting terrorism. The Homeland Security Act combined 22 federal entities to form the Department of Homeland Security, which has a mission to keep the homeland safe and secure. During the department's first several years, divisions and agencies have been juggled between directorates, but its mission has remained the same.

Undoubtedly, like 9/11 and Katrina, disasters will occur that uncover holes and weaknesses within homeland security. Building a safer nation will take time and patience, but more important, vision and dedication. As years pass, the nation takes steps further and further away from September 11. Already, people have forgotten the threats and have begun to complain about inconveniences they once thought were necessary. The DHS is not solely responsible for national security. Homeland security falls into the hands of every institution and community and every American.

GLOSSARY

ally   A country, person, or group joined with another or others for a common purpose.

anarchy   The complete absence of government.

colonialism   The system or policy by which a country maintains foreign colonies, especially in order to exploit them economically.

Cold War   The ideological conflict between the United States and the Soviet Union during the second half of the twentieth century; the conflict never led to direct military action.

communism   Any economic theory or system based on the ownership of all property by the community as a whole.

counterterrorism   Action intended to counteract or suppress terrorism.

domestic terrorism   An act of violence committed by a group without foreign influence or support in violation of the criminal laws of the United States, intended to intimidate the public or influence government policies.

dragnet   An organized system or network for gathering or catching criminals or others wanted by the authorities.

espionage   The use of spies to obtain information about the plans and activities of a foreign government or a competing company.

first responder   A certified emergency, medical, or law enforcement officer who is the first to arrive at an accident or a disaster scene.

ideology   The doctrines, opinions, or ways of thinking of an individual or group or class, specifically the body of ideas on which a particular political, economic, or social system is based.

infrastructure   The basic installations and facilities on which a community depends, such as roads, schools, power plants, and transportation and communications systems.

sabotage   Destructive or obstructive action taken by a civilian or an enemy agent to hinder a nation's war effort.

sanction   A coercive measure, like an economic blockade, usually taken by several nations together to force another country considered to have violated international law to end the violation.

secede   To withdraw from an organization, such as a federation or a political party.

socialism   Any of various economic or political theories that advocate collective or government ownership and administration of the means of production and the distribution of goods.

superpower   Any of the few top world powers competing with one another for international influence.

BIBLIOGRAPHY

Bullock, Jane A., George D. Haddow, Damon Coppola, Erdem Ergin, Lissa Westerman, and Sarp Yeletaysi. *Introduction to Homeland Security*. New York: Elsevier Butterworth-Heine-mann, 2005.

Clarke, Richard A. *Against All Enemies: Inside America's War on Terror*. New York: Free Press, 2004.

Corbin, Jane. *Al-Qaeda: The Terror Network That Threatens the World*. New York: Thunder's Mouth Press, 2002.

Hillyard, Michael J. *Homeland Security and the Need for Change*. Chula Vista, Calif.: Aventine Press, LLC, 2003.

Kean, Thomas and Lee H. Hamilton. *The 9/11 Commission Report: Final Report of the National Commission on Terror-ist Attacks Upon the United States*. New York: St. Martin's Paperbacks, 2004.

Longman, Jere. *Among the Heroes: United Flight 93 and the Passengers and Crew Who Fought Back*. New York: Harper Collins Publishers, 2002.

Sauter, Mark A. and James Jay Carafano. *Homeland Security: A Complete Guide to Understanding, Preventing, and Surviving Terrorism*. New York: McGraw-Hill Companies Inc., 2005.

9-11: A Tribute. Ferndown Gardens, Cobham, Surrey, United Kingdom: TAJ Books Limited, 2002.

FURTHER READING

Campbell, Geoffrey. *A Vulnerable America: An Overview of National Security*. New York: Lucent Books, 2004.

Egendorf, Laura. *National Security*. Farmington Hills, Mich.: Greenhaven Press, 2002.

Evans, Fred. *Maritime and Port Security*. Philadelphia, Pa.: Chelsea House, 2004.

Gerdes, Louise I. *The Patriot Act: Opposing Viewpoints*. Farmington Hills, Mich.: Greenhaven Press, 2005.

Hurley, Jennifer. *Weapons of Mass Destruction: Opposing Viewpoints*. Farmington Hills, Mich.: Greenhaven Press, 1999.

Stinson, Doug. *Protecting the Nation's Borders*. Farmington Hills, Mich.: Greenhaven Press, 2005.

Web Sites

Department of Homeland Security Web Site
www.dhs.gov

Inside 9/11: National Geographic
www9.nationalgeographic.com/channel/inside911/

Oklahoma City National Memorial Web Site
www.oklahomacitynationalmemorial.org

Ready Kids: Department of Homeland Security
www.ready.gov/kids/home.html

The White House: Homeland Security
www.whitehouse.gov/infocus/homeland/index.html

PICTURE CREDITS

INDEX

ABOUT THE AUTHOR

RACHEL A. KOESTLER-GRACK has worked as an editor and a writer of nonfiction books since 1999. During her career, she has worked extensively on historical topics, ranging from the Middle Ages to the Colonial era to the civil rights movement. In addition, she has written numerous biographies on a variety of historical and contemporary figures. Koestler-Grack lives with her husband and daughter on a hobby farm near Glencoe, Minnesota.